T0083663

PRACTICING the TRUTH

PRACTICING the TRUTH

POEMS

Ellery Akers

Autumn House Press

PITTSBURGH

"Autumn House Press" and "Autumn House" are registered trademarks owned by Autumn House Press, a nonprofit corporation whose mission is the publication and promotion of poetry and other fine literature.

Autumn House Press Staff
Michael Simms: Founder and Editor-in-Chief
Eva Simms: Co-Founder and President
Giuliana Certo: Managing Editor
Christine Stroud: Associate Editor
Chris Duerr: Assistant Editor
Alison Taverna: Intern
Sharon Dilworth, John Fried: Fiction Editors
J.J. Bosley, CPA: Treasurer
Anne Burnham: Fundraising Consultant
Michael Wurster: Community Outreach Consultant
Jan Beatty: Media Consultant
Heather Cazad: Contest Consultant
Michael Milberger: Tech Crew Chief

Autumn House Press receives state arts funding support through a grant from the Pennsylvania Council on the Arts, a state agency funded by the Commonwealth of Pennsylvania, and the National Endowment for the Arts, a federal agency.

ISBN: 978-1-938769-04-7
Library of Congress Control Number: 2014954404

Contents

PRACTICING the TRUTH

1

The Word That is a Prayer

One thing you know when you say it:
all over the earth people are saying it with you;
a child blurting it out as the seizures take her,
a woman reciting it on a cot in a hospital.
What if you take a cab through the Tenderloin:
at a street light, a man in a wool cap,
yarn unraveling across his face, knocks at the window;
he says, *Please.*
By the time you hear what he's saying,
the light changes, the cab pulls away,
and you don't go back, though you know
someone just prayed to you the way you pray.
Please: a word so short
it could get lost in the air
as it floats up to God like the feather it is,
knocking and knocking, and finally
falling back to earth as rain,
as pellets of ice, soaking a black branch,
collecting in drains, leaching into the ground,
and you walk in that weather every day.

My Mother, Sunbathing

She got up around noon,
hung over, bruised where my father hit her,
tore off the black satin Sleepwell mask she slept in,
had her maid pull back the curtain,
ate her one egg, one slice of toast, and got dressed:
a bikini. She lay on a lounger, oiled, eyes closed,
fished around the patio for her tumbler,
found it, stirred the ice with her finger,
then lifted it, eyes still shut, to her mouth.
I remember the knobs of corns on her toes, her high, pale arches,
and how, from time to time, she'd flop her wrist into the bushes
and absentmindedly pat the roses beside her,
and though I knocked out the Japanese beetles
that rolled in the petals and chewed their way through,
I doubt if she ever noticed.

Most of the time she was lying face down,
her blonde hair falling through the slats:
I was never quite sure if she wanted to be seared
or forgiven; it was almost a dream she was dreaming
not by night, but by day.

Eight hours: it was all she ever wanted.
Each day she turned a shade darker
so that by the end of summer she was bronze, almost black,
though the palms of her hands were still white.
If she was standing in a shadow in the living room, you could
    barely see her:
just a shock of bleached hair and a flash of teeth.

Drunk, in the dark, in the cool, her skin radiating heat
and gleaming with oil, she looked alien to the room,
and even to the earth, as if she wanted to go back to the hot core
of the star, which would deliver her.

Practicing the Truth

1

I've spent my life watching trees
because trees take root and fasten,
unlike my father, the way he swerved so often
into the rage he couldn't feel as a child,
listening to *his* father slide the belt buckle open;
though they're dead now, and what they did
is shoveled alongside them,
like dark shells of bees, their stings used up.

2

But rocks do not lift and throw themselves.
The grass remains hooked to the earth.
Showers of blackbirds fall and keep on falling
and do not turn into scattershot or buckshot:
the slope stays put, the pond stays put,
and does not fly or shed its wings.

Doves moan, but they should moan
when the hawk splits the back of the neck
with one slice of its talons.
The shrike nails the vole to the cactus spine,
but this is the way of shrikes, the *butcher birds:*
they've been doing it since the beginning.

3

He always used to switch on the lamp
when I was reading, and once was late
because he stopped to feed a bone-thin Airedale
nosing about outside a restaurant.
When we went to the shore, he'd lift my sister and me
over the mats of kelp
into the clear water, where we would swim.

But later, it was as if an eclipse darkened the room
when he entered; the light went dead,
and everything shut down
except for the need to climb into a smaller body
and another one, still smaller, and all of them calling out *Don't.*

That didn't work, and after a while
I would simply drift toward the ceiling
and look back at my body:
a meteorite dropped on the bed, a chunk of ore,
rubbled, like the ones I'd seen in the planetarium,
with zircon and black glass.

So that I'm still only certain of a few things:
that the Archer follows the Arrow every night,
that the Eagle follows the Swan;
that the planets are strung along the ecliptic and stay there,
beautiful as the names of trees: sassafras, box elder, alder,
as my name means alder,
white in the mountains, red on the coast,
its roots reach down a dozen feet or more for water.

4

When I was older, I'd slog through wet fields at night,
the Passumpsic spilling over its knuckles of rocks and bottles,
and the stars would stretch out their charts,
the coarse grasses parted in front of me—
my pant legs sopping, flapping against my ankles—
but I always knew something here
could heal me: these slow envelopes of cumulus,
the vegetative sway of sap in the stalk,
water sluicing in the trunks of trees,
extracting what's needed from the ground,
nitrates, phosphates, long shafts of water
pumped up into xylem and phloem.

Tonight I lie on the bridge that smells of creosote, as always.
Capella flashes scarlet and turquoise in the smudge on the
        horizon.
Cassiopeia, Andromeda prick out their cold nets over my head,
their light too old and pale to fall on my face,
though for a minute I can almost feel it:
a thin glaze sent from millions of miles.

What Rises in the Sea at Night Rises in Dreams

> By the time the last light has faded from the sky, the surface
> layers of the water, so empty before, are a teeming soup of
> planktonic animal life.
>
> *The Life of the Ocean*, N.J. Berrill

Every night the largest migration of animals in the world
rises while we sleep—
arrow worms clear as glass, comb jellies,
salps. When the first sting of sun
strikes the water, they sink back down.
And while I fall asleep, some unlived life
floats toward me,
or starved parts of myself I pushed down
rise and scan my eyelids
for some kind of recognition
before they sink into the steep drop-off of the brain.
One night I dreamt I heard a golden tone;
a bell rang, but it was a bell made of krill,
climbing out of blackness so cold it stank of cold.
And in the sea, too, there are bells of jellyfish,
rafts of plankton, pulsing with light, that swim to the surface
and rock back and forth.
Fishermen know this:
they shoot their drift nets at night
into a sheen of dinoflagellates:
the wake of their boats "shines like silver fire;"
you can read a newspaper if you lean over the bow.
One man wrote his signature on a Pyrosoma
and saw his name flash in letters of fire,
and when he went to sleep, he dreamt
that deep in the sea, where rain doesn't penetrate,

or the sound of rain,
his name was climbing towards him
through the benthic cold:
night after night it kept trying to reach him
through the deep speech of the sea.

Fifth Grade

That Christmas vacation, Serena Allen invited me over and asked
    me to tell her a secret.
She was excited, so I came up with a lie about this boy I liked,
I'd watched him that summer jackknifing into the water from a
    dock,
but Serena pumped me for details, *Did you like him, did you kiss
    him,*
did you want to kiss him, then pulled out a tape recorder she'd
    hidden under her bed.
She'd been taping it all, said she'd play it in front of the class,
and I got into my bulky coat and trudged home in the snow.
As I look back, it's the endurance that moves me, the lack of
    surprise:
I *knew* people were like this, they would hurt you and shame
    you, that was their nature.
I remember how snow dissolved as it rushed into drains,
it was like secrecy itself, so thick and packed no one could see you.
It wasn't my feeling for the boy that was important—
I don't even remember his name—it was the sense of betrayal,
how she'd trapped my voice like a bird in that box under her bed:
she could summon it at the flick of her hand, and it would fly.

Good

1

When my mother fell face down into her salad at the table,
or dug her nails into my arm and said, "It's all your fault,"
or when Miss Harper, with her knob of hair,
threw our turtles out the window,
and they turned in the air, their stumpy legs pumping
before their shells hit the pavement five floors down,
I expected the world to be violent and unpredictable,
and what you could do about it was to be good.

I never cried, or talked back, the way my sister did,
I held on to each rule as if it were a bridge I could cross
and get to the other side:
when the door banged behind us in music class,
everyone turned around except for me,
because Miss Drake said not to,
and when the doctor slid the cold otoscope into my ear
and pushed his wire in, I didn't say anything.
I tried to understand what was required.

2

One Halloween, the older kids hazed the fifth graders;
they set up a tunnel, turned off the lights,
and pushed us through: they brushed us with mops,
they bit us and grabbed us
with rubber gloves filled with ice and coated with lard
and all the time one of them kept screaming and flashing a green
light

so we could see a glimpse of black lips and teeth,
an eye, a mouth filled with blood. They told me later
I was no fun—I didn't scream and run with the others,
I just walked through, slowly,
as if I could walk that way into the Antarctic
where penguins stood the cold for months on end—
they stood it, we watched it in the movie:
they had blades of ice on their feathers,
they kept their eggs warm on their feet
so they'd hatch in the blizzard.
That's the kind of birds they were: they were good.

You Talk to Yourself About Being Alone

You know the punctuation of loneliness,
knocking together its grammar in the dark:
such small rules it has.

In your house, the rooms fill with your name,
layered like felt on the walls.

Not solitude, which is different, deep as humus on a forest floor,
loneliness is diffuse:

At a party, you turn around, and there it is, padding behind you,
laying its damp glove on your shoulder,
and it asks you to find a place for it at last:

How it has been a companion, independence its close sister,
sponging the hours with its stained cloth,
leading you past the avenues of glare, where no one wants to go.

You are an expert in its slow, moldering weather.
And you are sure the climate is different somewhere else:
like a sailor, day after day, under a lid of grey sky
who finally sees a strip of blue
and islands, macaws of all colors, in pairs.

Leaving Her Body

1

And didn't anyone want to stop that child
as she opened the ceiling and flew out
as if he'd flipped a nickel on a bet
and it just kept spinning out of the world?
Didn't anyone see her flare out
over smoke, over starlings,
their thin hearts beating even faster than hers
as he threw her into the air
and she sped towards the Dipper, the Pole?

2

How could he let one of his own
unhook from the world so early,
drift past slate roofs and chimneys
into the ravine of the stars, like one of those satellites
that ticks and spanks along on its shiny tin
out of the solar system, into the Coalsack, the night?

The Shouting Match with My Mother: at Sixteen

Afterwards, all I knew
was I had to get to something large and cold that didn't lie,
so I pedaled to the sea,
the rusted spokes of my bike creaking with every turn of the
      wheel.
I lifted the broken chain-link fence,
stepped past logs and beer cans,
stripped to my bathing suit,
and threw myself into the water.
I liked the way the salt stung,
and even the way strings of seaweed
brushed my feet, though when they looped around me,
I kicked them away.
With every stroke I was getting farther
from Cliff Break, the house my mother grew up in
and was broken in, a girl who could see the years rust
and the rust wash in with the scum of foam
in that cove where her father fished for her soul
as if it was his, and hooked it, and took it
so that I never saw it, only what was left:
rage, ash, and bourbon.
I swam so far the lights on the shore
looked like gold bees, and then like pollen.
I wanted the cold, and the shock of cold
and the salt that crossed back and forth between my teeth,
I wanted the sea to slide over my body
and rinse the anger out of my hair,
but I finally turned back,
sidestroked to the beach,

and stared, as I always did, at the stars,
the only connection I could think of back then,
one radiant cold statement, then millions of miles,
nail after nail,
each one hammered next to each other,
divided by distance, as they should be, like mother and daughter.

2

What I Do

I drive on country roads, where kangaroo rats shoot across the blacktop and leap into bushes, where feral cats streak through fields and cows lift their heads at the sound of the car but don't stop chewing, where horses' manes blow in the wind and cheatgrass blows, and grapes are strapped to stakes as if they have been crucified

I drive past the Soledad liquor store, where the neon starts, and the argon, past the Ven-A-Mexico restaurant, past fields full of white hair—it's just water spurting across all that lettuce—and a jackrabbit runs and freezes, and digger pines stand on either side of the road and the car plunges over cattleguards, rattling—

Sometimes I listen to the earth—it has a sound: deep inside, the garnets churning

Sometimes I listen to the birds: the sharp *whir* in the air as a swallow veers over my head, as a wren flies, panting, carrying a twig longer than she is, and by this time I can tell from the sounds of their wings, without looking, whether a titmouse just passed—*flutter*—a raven—*thwack, thwack*—an eagle—*shud, shud, shud*—big wet sheets flapping on a laundry line

I paint: I draw: I swab gesso on canvas, rinsing the brushes again and again, as paler and paler tints go down the drain

I cook, I shell peas, breaking open the pods at the veins with a snap: I take vitamins—all the hard, football-shaped pills—sometimes they get stuck in my gullet and I panic and think what a modern way to die, they'll come and find my dead, perfectly healthy body

I pay attention to willows: I sniff the river
I collect otoliths, and the small ear bones of seals
I notice a dead mouse on the path, its tail still curled, its snout
    eaten away by ants

So that although I've forgotten what John and I said to each other
outside the airport, I remember the cedar waxwings chattering and
lighting on the telephone wires, the clipped stiff grass and how
sharp it was against my thighs as the waxwings flashed by

Bather in the night, the soap slides next to me in the tub
phone dialer when I'm scared, and want to hear Peter's voice, or
    Valerie's or Barbara's,
Xeroxer, the faint green light pulses over and over,
repeating my name as my poems flick by,
and the machine spits out copy after copy
swimmer, slow breaststroke, hand over hand, kick

I stand at the podium in my jacket, always a jacket to cover up my
breasts so I don't feel so naked

I see my therapist, my words fill up the room, the past is enormous,
I steer towards anger and practice anger as if it were Italian, I
throw stones at the canyon wall and yell and sometimes a clump
of shale falls down and a spider races out

I watch tadpoles and water striders: once, six miles in at Mud
Lake, some drunken men, a rifle crack, I ran the whole way to the
car—

I come back to Soledad: at night, plume moths and geometrid
moths flatten themselves against the motel windows, looking like
chips of bark, and in the morning a starling teeters across the trash

bin—pecking at Cellophane, walking over the Styrofoam containers from McDonald's. A man who looks scared says, "Good Morning, Ma'am," as he throws away more Styrofoam, and I drive under the cool overpass where pigeons nest every year, flapping up into steel slots, as trucks go past with their loads—

Needing to pile up silence outside me and within me
the silence underneath the bulbs of zigadene, stinkhorn, and
blood-red saprophytes—
as the minutes open into parachutes that fall and fall again

The Parallel and Not Inferior World

While the young man strokes his lover's arm
the wren lifts her cloaca

while he kisses her
the leaves are exploding out of their sheaths

while she kisses him back
they are speaking all the green verbs they know:

they are leaning out of their stems and lunging towards the sun,
they are breathing for us, chinquapin, kinnikinnick,
they are moving their hinges in the wind
so that briars break out of their secrecy
and tongues and vines of wild cucumber wipe away gravel from
    the rock,
and sticktight and bindweed let the sun strike them again and
    again,
and morning glories unravel all over the hot fence:
they are pressing their membranes to the corridors of the exact
    world,
they are inhaling, exhaling, asking, *"What is separate?"*

Lesions

Starfish have been dying by the millions along the U.S. west coast . . . the arms of infected starfish begin to twist and then "crawl" away from the creature's body until they tear off . . .

—*Science Mail Online*

Whenever a species gets stubbed out like this,
I feel the border of our lives is fraying:
the map of the sea yanked blank in one corner,
becoming a pocket of nothing,
as in *Where do you keep your nothing? Here.*
Sometimes I think we're holding the diameter
of the earth in our hands—
an elastic band, stretched tight—
and we're living in the years
before it snaps back
and tosses animals and trees and us away.
Maybe we should write a letter to those people of the future:
Here is the earth. Love it for us.
It's hard to believe, but we loved it, too.

Moonlight: Gabilan Mountains

It's bright up there, with its craters, shining by earthshine:
but down here it's a sting of light between the buttes,
a shawl dropped onto cheatgrass and chia;
it's cooling the grass, dulling the knives,
calling the leaves
to forget all they've learned, to go back to the place
before the names started.
I can almost believe metal hasn't been extracted:
aluminum, tin, tungsten, steel—
no one sharpens his saw, no one stands with his rifle.
A shelf of shadows blurs across the road,
and that digger pine, and that old blunt snag,
and live oak and blue oak
that pricked the air this morning
and looked crisp, starched
begin to dissolve
and a log that was perfectly solid stains and drifts away
and a couple of swifts twang across the hill
as if someone were whipping the air with a wet rope
and the moon smokes across gravel:
cliffs kneel, rocks cool,
trunks give up their heat.
Nothing solid exists, no bones or edges,
even the boulders blur, and the bridges,
and just as I'm beginning to believe
it's not true that everything is born into the world
to be torn by someone or something,
an owl, long-eared or barn, cuts across the night,
sharpening the saw of its cry
as voles stiffen in their tunnels of grass.

Hook

One year a general
packs the dead arithmetic in a drawer—
all the subtractions, divisions.
The next year, vines cover the bunkers.
The brain resumes its starbursts of rehearsal.
The heart leaps under the defibrillator.
The bone eases into its socket.
Skin grows back. Scars fade. Eyes clear.
Look at the trees at the burn, six years later.
Look at the sprout on a hay bale
on a truck. Look at the woman who was raped,
had her hands cut off in a creek:
she's getting married.
The choir sings. The bride smiles.
The groom slips a ring on her hook.

Insects at Dusk

You can see how every night is like this for them:
the gradual cooling, the tremendous effort to walk,
how darkness abrades them, how their life leaks
out of them, and they have to wait.
Next morning, stiffened,
they move slowly towards noon:
they are replete with gold: they don't think of anything
but gathering what they need.
The whole day ripens in front of them.
But at night, again, they have to weaken.
Their legs lock. Their mouths refuse to open.
Their lives are spent in diminishment and preparation:
over and over, they are learning to die.

The Tree Speaks to its Seedling:
About Light, About Birds

Open your hands, now. Let them be flat.
Let them be glad. Let the halls and cells
be opened to receive the King.
In the night: wait. In the shade: wait.
Also, the moon will come, with its stale cold.
From time to time there will come the small bumpers,
the birds. They are welcome.
They will scrape you, they will brush against you,
they will lock you with their talons.
They are in a hurry: we are not in a hurry.
They will bring sticks, and lay them on your arms,
and sit on them. We think perhaps
it is a form of worship. Perhaps the sticks
are their King.
In the daytime: steer. In the night: store.
Remember: always steer towards the King.

Long Distance: England

> I think the transmission of the human voice is much more
> nearly at hand than I had supposed.
>
> —Alexander Graham Bell

Somewhere along the line
hail strikes the wire
that holds your voice,
and that wire,
slung between two poles,
sways in the wind.
I think of the men who stood in a steel bucket
or climbed those poles.
I think of the poles themselves,
stripped of leaves, standing among live trees
smelling of sap and chlorophyll:
spike after spike sunk in the wood
and still its cells remember the breeze,
though bolted and coated with creosote.
Bell is in this call, too:
his patience during the day,
trying one magnetic strip after another;
his doubt at night,
looking at the moon through a window,
inhaling the smell of dusty cretonne.
And somewhere back in the forties
is a bored woman wearing a hairnet in a radio transmitter factory,
her blouse stained with crescents of sweat
as she places knob after knob on a conveyor belt.
This copper was dug from the ground, from the bald scrape
of an open-pit mine, a hill turned to powder,
and so in this call are the miners and smelters,
the odor of packed ore dumped on a truck.

While I'm telling you how much I miss you,
a falcon, his talons wrapped around my voice,
is picking off bird lice.
While you tell me how much you miss me,
a rough-legged hawk clasps the wire—
feathers lift on his thighs
as he tears off a gopher haunch, and stops and eats, and tears
     again.
Our voices course through hundreds of talons
before they plunge into the ocean, where fish hang above your
     name
or bump the cable, and kelp loops ropes around my questions,
     your answers:
spliced together as we are
so I can speak to you; so you can speak to me.

The Oak Gall

The wasp holds her abdomen over the leaf,
wings throbbing, swings her ovipositor around,
and stings. Then it starts.
This leaf will never be the same as the others.
It will never pack exact light into cells.
Slowly it will become deformed.
Slowly it will build what it was never meant to build,
a crown, or a blade, or a long pink thorn.
The cells have gone wild from toxins,
but the rest of the leaf does not want to know:
it just wants to go back to its factories of chlorophyll.
The scar insists, so the leaf folds cells around it
and a green wall begins to grow.
Slowly the wasp egg receives its instructions
and turns into chitin. The wasp breaks out
and veers into the world. The gall stays on the leaf.
Only a hole remains where the wasp bit its way out.
The leaf is beautiful, in its way.
It's got this mad cathedral at its center.

The Night Bride

To own the night is to lie on my back letting the stars come in, black by blink black—

The trees smell different at night, darker, full of loam, as I walk under the moon, trusting reversal, and I feel the noon alien as if it were beating some gong into a forehead of rock—

But I want to be a day bride, too, claim the day, step forward into the glare of speech so that everything I discarded at night—every seed in its dry capsule—throws itself into that blue elevator and floats—

Though the day moon hangs in the plain old day—just some white plate on a shelf in the warehouse of morning—

and I look for night to cauterize me, hide me in its cool calendar.

I belong to the night—I'm in love with its closures—leaves shut down, chloroplasts—an oak carved into form—everything reduced to core, trunk and crown—and I stand on the crown, a day blooming, blowing from under the earth, every tree trunk glazed with its allowable moon.

Trying to Call the Soul Back Into the Body

1

Swallows are *meant* to be in the air.
They turn at some blue intersection we can't see:
they are our alternates.
We are not meant to race; we are not meant to fly.
We are clumsy because earth is clumsy,
mud slides downhill, hooks of filaree stick to our socks.
We pull ourselves across the world
carrying our hearts—systole, diastole:

You think your body would strap itself into a metal box
and race down a road painted with broken yellow lines
if it weren't for the mind, that radio with its bracelets of static?

2

I want to honor every sloth, every porcupine,
every badger scuffing the ground with its dust-colored arms,
I want to praise the dumbness of leaves,
the whole dank world unwrapping,
ferns unfolding in their own time.
I want to honor that whale playing one slow joke after another,
the joke with the fluke,
the one with the fin and the spout.
I want to make rare, offshore mistakes.
I want to praise the body, with its feet padding across the years,
and the bones, falling forward as I walk,
catching themselves, and falling again.

As if they know, those bones, where they belong.

The body slowly revolving in its harness of earth.
The earth slowly revolving in its harness of air.

3

Abuse: Reconsidering the Strategy of Silence

1

There is secrecy in locks,
calling all night their ammonia song, *stay out.*
There is evasion in spoons,
curving away so gracefully as they do.

There is secrecy in fish that carry their young in their mouths,
in a spider climbing out of a sink drain and climbing back again
into the dark pipes in the wall.

Did you ever see a secret that wasn't a fraction?
Numerator, denominator, that slash.
Did you ever kiss someone who had a secret
strapped to her mouth, and it entered your mouth with its chill?

Then you know about the lock, and the cash,
about silence flanneling your life,
muffled like snow on the windows,
pads and lids and coverings of all kinds,
vials stoppered,
latches, stitches, and velour.

2

I wanted to be safe as an inch is safe
while a mile lunges out,
throwing itself down the road.
Cars slam back and forth across it.
What happens to an inch? Nothing.

3

But I don't want to stand in the rain and be the rain.
I don't want to be invisible: silver: excoriate.
I don't want to be cancelled by snow,
by promises, by wadded Kleenex, abashed and abraded,
washed by shame or erased by water.

I want to walk under the sky with its black lock of silence:
count the stars, with all their keys.

She Always Dreams of Escape

The way snow hardens against her feet as she travels:
the signal flashes—the trackers follow,
I'll never get away, she thinks.

Now she begins to run, a mistake: they will hold her down,
her mouth full of snow.

Remember how the night hardened its glance
and did nothing to help her?

She was alone except for snow
as it fell on the ice coating the river,

But snow doesn't tell the truth, snow lies,
covering the names of things,
blunting the spiked shapes of metal
concealed in its folds.

The picture coming clearer in her body
as if she were both camera and developer,
the blizzard of years
becoming less blurred in the enlarger:

Here is the photograph: he is bending over her.
She sees what it is, where it begins.

The Colors She Keeps Painting

Black for the shackle, red for the bolt
black for the barge on the black Black Sea
black for the stammer, red for the shout
black for the way he leaned over me

Black for the nostrils, red for the lips
black for the way I stood singed in the dark
red for the roof of the mouth

Black for the dial, red for the wall
red for the liar, pants on fire
black to drowse, and red to wake
red for the crotch and the roof of the mouth

Black for silence: for refusal: for smoldering
for the orchard scorched after fire
stumps turned black, earth turned black and smoking
red for the tongue: the mistake: the diagnosis

Black for stitches, for the weight of silence
though some words are black, too, like No
and Stop It is red of course
black for the iris of his eye
black for the grackle, red for the cardinal
black for the black-backed gull who stamped in the sand
as I packed the bandages and brought them back

Black for the pencil, black for the lead
black for graphite, for lignite, for anthracite
black for words printed on the page next to each other

red for the red *ta-rah, ta-rah* of the trumpet
red for the woman being washed and washed in the river
red for danger, red to stop
black for the elevator that drops and drops
black for the cough in the night, and the coal
black as he stood over me with his hand for a hatchet
black for the cricket, the talon, the nail

Red for flags that crease in the wind and slap and slap
red for knees pressed into the earth
black for the palm and the slap of the palm
for the shut sound it makes all night in the room

Red for the red roof of the mouth

For the Child I Was

1

I keep coming back to that room—
the wallpaper with its shackled roses.

How I wish I could lean back into the past
and stroke my own hair,

but what could I say except *live:*
watch the leaves;
their oars will row you into the future.

2

I can see her in bed, patient as wood
stroking her sateen comforter, flashes, sparks in the dark,
saying, "Our Father, who art in heaven," for all the good it did,
and outside, the city clanking, a great heart made of iron,
snow falling in the streets, like blood in the body,
silently, with no evil intent.

My Father's Geology Lesson

Look at that daughter and her father.
They seem happy. He is lacing up her skates.
She will skate for him until she is cold.
He tells her that the stuff that blazes in this rock
is not gold, but fool's gold, mica, hammered out
when the black rock slammed through the dirt.
Though it's so pretty, it's nothing. He pounds his gloves
to keep warm, a patient man explaining the difference
between what's real and what's not real.
You can see that something is shining between them: it's his
    kindness,
a sheet of foil blazing in front of his body,
like gold, fool's gold, mica.

You Ask What Saved Me

To be born in New York in 1946 in a room
where light sifts through the slats of your crib
and a man rummages across your body
teaches you to make your way alone. You learn to listen.
You notice the clang of the lid on the ice bucket
and the sound of the ice pick
as your mother chips her way towards her scotch.
You lean out the window to watch the parade,
how it starts—the first xylophone girl as she struts down the
    avenues,
tassels bouncing on her boots—how it ends, the last cleanup
    machine
spraying water, knocking Cracker Jack boxes into the sewer.

Here is the Boston street where I strapped on plastic boots
to walk in the slush, past scraped walls of snow;
here is the snow coming down like bees,
and Orion, one more time
his belt pricked out, and his wild white throat,
his two dogs snapping at his heels across the sky
as I walked into spring
past the drugstore window and its isinglass.

I am younger now than I was in 1948,
the year I left for the first time, drifted into the sky
and came back changed and thinner,
my name held shut between my teeth.
It took me years to get out of New York, out of Boston,
to travel across one bleached and rotting log after another,

lean down to watch garter snakes wrinkle into the water
or count scale insects, massed on a branch,
or drowned flies piling up on loose scarves of algae.

Here are the next twenty years as I lay on my back,
brushing away gravel from under my shoulder blades,
here are the stars that swarm into the cold every night,
three nails in the Eagle, six in the Swan:
my butane stove dividing the hours with its blue flame
as I watched the Lion, the Square.

I can still remember that silver purse I sniffed for its tarnish
in my mother's closet, next to her pearl-colored pumps.
Here is an owl I made for her in school—
shoved into her drawer full of trash and cigarette butts—
staring back at me with eyes
pressed out by my thumbs.
Here are the quilted bed jackets she wore to cover her bruises,
her hair smelling of Lucky Strikes.

I can still hear the sound of quarters sliding into my pocket
as I wiped off tables at Cronin's;
I can still hear the sound of cars grating across the steel teeth of
     the bridge
as I walked past the elementary school, paper hands stuck to
     windows
as if kids were down there in the cellar, signaling to be let out.

The Said Floats on the Unsaid

Talk to me. What isn't spoken
becomes weeds lining the roads,
thistles tossing their seeds in the air,
white spokes
quiet as the breath of the dead
saying over and over
what was hoarded, what was never said.

Spoon

My mother was born with a silver spoon in her mouth and
    became all spoon:
polished every day, she lay back in the silverware drawer on
    satin.
Spoon of Southern belle, spoon of geisha,
spoon tapping the baby on the fontanelle;
spoon that raised an internal silver alarm.

Curved as she was, she lay powerless beside the rest of the
    silverware,
married to liquid as they were to meat,
serving up soup:
it's what she was made for.
At the table the men with their serrations and tines
stabbed their decisions beside her.

Like it or not, you are made in the shape of your mother:
she is the mouth inside your mouth.
Poured into a mold, scooped out so early,
there was nothing left of her but a thin tongue of silver.

What My Mother Carries

She's piled cases of cigarettes and boxes of monogrammed stationery, drapes and mahogany furniture, kilos of blockage and seepage, and hoists them on her shoulders like Atlas, but she is no Atlas, only an anorexic with her hair burnt off by peroxide over the years.

With the thin bones of her hand she is holding up rafts of drugstores, whole city blocks, statuary, the Mint with its presses churning out dollars.

There is secrecy in the air around her, wigs on wigstands, bottles of Ambien and Ativan, dresses with matching pumps.

What you blot out begins to shine, a sheet of tinfoil: you'd think it would be a dark cellar, but it's a spark caught in the throat. She throws years at it, bottles of scotch, bracelets, in an effort to blot it out.

You'd think it would be dark by now, but it stays under her tongue, an atom of silver. It's down to one photon, but it still goes on shining, she will die with it padded and clouded, flashing its spokes into the dark.

Rage

Sometimes I think it will never go away, how I'm full of rage the way a car is full of radio noise, men packed in the front seat and back, arms out the windows, hands drumming on the Chevy doors, the car turning around, purposefully now, the men getting out, kicking, throwing, breaking bottles, hand them anything, a body, they want to break it, hit it, feel the body topple and make the sound a body makes when it will never stand up again. It has been the dark package I wanted to return, it has been the fuel, the cords of wood, pig iron, slabs, freight, pitchforks full of hay still smelling faintly of the fields, stones and magma: lava beginning to pour, leakage, breakage, storage, and slag, the inferno contained in a Bunsen burner, in a snip of a backpacking stove hooked up to a butane canister with its pinched-off spurts of flame that hiss under the stars with their flares and engines, the galaxy tossing itself farther and farther from that collision of particles we come from, elements starting to fuse, thudding and crashing together, electrons, lead chunking together, bismuth chunking, wolfram, beryllium, zinc, *chunk chunk chunk* out there where we can just see the white curtain of nerves flashing, where it started, where it led to—car doors slamming, smell of burning rubber, the slang and the tongue, trucks loaded with rifles, the whole cargo with its black holes pulling you in, sucking you back to the original dark blank, the way it slams forward, backward, get that man off that child, stop him, break him, make him pay.

The Hive

Sometimes she thinks God
is a dark glove
and holds each of us
night after night,
until at last we're poured into gold cells and sealed.

But that was the way honey was pressed into combs,
from alfalfa and clover,
dances in the hive,
bees that caulk every crevice with varnish.

She takes off that buzz helmet of nerves
and lays out honeycombs—
spokes of light
traveling from one amber ingot to another.

But she remembers that fist,
and the stings,
when she and the bees lay down together.

The Question of Forgiveness
Comes up Again in Winter

Because I took everything hard, that's the way I took snow:
slush and crusts by the curb—
at eight, bundled in a snow suit
I blundered through those clumps, as if *No* had fallen
during the night, and the stems of *Yes*
were too weak to protest:
snow cancelled everything under it,
it was like secrecy, denial, it covered the street
with a stainless intention, it made inhalation
a shock; it slipped across the hill
like the mean slow smile of a father, sure of his power,
mesmerized blackbirds so their eyes went blank,
blotted out a field and replaced it with veto.

At twenty I got my first job in snow.
It was a Vermont town,
stiff porches, tight churches,
chapped lips, Vaseline, discouragement,
turning always to the clamp of winter;
I listened to shovels clang as they hit pavement,
plows shunting snow into loaves streaked with dirt.
Snow made lace out of horse dung, erased the spokes of a bicycle.
To stay there, you had to love snow.

Every night snow buried the streets
and left roads in ruin.
I thought snow was related to ruin,
but now I know there's no end to sharpness in the world,
and if snow drifts and folds,
one white blur, and then another,

I can see why:
sometimes you don't want to remember,
you want to forget. Snow can do it for you.
That's what snow does.

4

The Naturalist in Love

I could listen all morning to an ash-throated flycatcher
as he gave off a cry like a sparkle of metal:
I could pick up racers, let their cool scales glide from hand to
    hand
and let them go:

So when I touch the curve of your ear
or the slope of your chest, I think *shell, moraine,*

I lift a strand of your hair
the way I used to lift a tiger moth trapped in a bathroom
and set it carefully on a leaf.

And when I slide my hand between your legs
I think of seaweed rolling in and out of the channel,
how kelp sways on top of the ocean,
all the blades spread across it, *Iridea, Gigartina.*

And sometimes, just before I cry out,
when your hand brushes lightly over my breast,
I remember that nivation hollow deep in the Steens
spilling over with steer's-head
cocked up to the sun in the snow:

How I could take an iris in my hand,
stare at the pistil, the anther: the way I used to bend over a plant,
slide its wet petals apart and notice the tracks laid down for the
    bees:
all the arrows, stripes, hairs that bend straight in:

So that when my leg touches yours on the creased sheets,
and I listen to you breathe as you fall asleep,
I lie back and inhale the dark red air of pollination,
packed into my body, petal by petal, attar of rose.

Looking Around

for Jim

I can still remember the night I went down to the river
on my shift break, with my clock,
the smell of crushed grass all around me
as I lay back in my waitress uniform and learned the stars
and they streamed into my chest with their order:

I can still remember that pencil factory I drove past every summer,
the huge splintery logs sprayed with water
as they slid onto conveyor belts, sawdust, hoses,
the smell of wet timber:

So what if I'm shattered: so are leaves,
and bent stalks, and rocks in the streambed
shattered into gravel:
look at the oaks, they're stung and stung;
every tree has a gall,
and the gall carries the wasp
and the branch carries the gall
and the bald taproot sniffing through the ground for water
carries the trunk of the oak:
that's how everything is carried, the way it should be,
the way that word he breathed in my ear once lined
the birth canal of his mother.

This time I don't want to rust, an iron streak on the blade of a
    knife,
I just want to say something largehearted and not bitter,
something about the way I raked his leg with my foot as we lay
    together.

Start over: as I pull on my jacket and walk under the moon
and the stars graze in the Coalsack
and the cormorant preens its bony black wing on the buoy
as it clanks in the troughs of the waves.

When I look at my life I can see a sane woman
walking through blunt grass:
I recognize myself by my scars
the way a heron knows the marsh
by the sunk wrecks of boats left to rust.

For My Sister, Who Died in Cosmetic Surgery

I don't love the freeway,
or the long necks of argon
that lean over my car,
or rain, filling up reservoirs
with its inches.
But since you died, I can't afford not to.
Because you'll never see this again.
There isn't itching where you are,
bits of eggshell stuck to dishes.

Six months, and you're buried beside our father,
which you wouldn't have liked.
But bones aren't afraid of bones.

Once I went into a gift shop,
came out, annoyed by lace, tea towels with ducks and hearts,
toilet paper stamped with daisies;
it made me want to see bandages, litter,
kelp covered with flies,
or gulls that eat anything.

They flap, screeching over a dune,
waddle towards a sandwich,
stalk and quarrel,
eyeing the greasy paper it's wrapped in,
even a plastic fork with its broken tines.

Yesterday I stepped in dog shit, tracked it over the rugs,
the kind of mistake you would never have made.
You hated it when I walked on the beach with you,

tracked tar in your car.
You threw out a blouse with a single stain.

Now you're there, stenciled into perfection,
your name carved into stone.
And I'm here. The day sprinkles its minutes across me.
I'm throwing out the garbage, crinkling a paper bag,
savoring the taste of water from a dented Dixie cup.

How you hated ruin:
how you felt it was a slur in the pores.
You threw money at it: scarves, shoes,
blusher, concealer, facelifts, pills.
How finally you threw your life at that dirty thing.

Grief Group

We get earaches,
weeping fits in stores,
read books that tell us
to whack pillows, throw rocks,
and all of us look nuts
in our various rooms
talking to air,
as if air could gather
its rearranged atoms
to make a mouth
to form just one word
back to us here, who need
that word, who want
that word, limping from the next world
on its crutches of bones.

One man, whose son
threw himself off a bridge
can't cross the bridge,
but his wife goes every week,
tosses wreaths.
They fall apart, roses blunder
into the water,
but she doesn't care,
it's what she has to do,
throw something into that hole in the river.

The Dead

The dead can't hear us when we talk:
there isn't air thin enough
for our words, solid as they are,
to get through that sieve light makes.
Static of light. Static of salt.

And we can't hear them, either:
sometimes they try to speak to us,
but when they open their mouths,
light comes out.

They are fishermen
who have stepped out of their oilskins
and dropped off the side of the boat,
naked, into the sea.

It's not that they can't hear our hoarse breath:
they can. But our grief sounds to them
like the barking of seals far off:
they can't remember what it means,
though they know they used to know.

Summer at Barbara's House

for my oldest friend

We loll on your patio
on cushions covered with dog hair,
sink into the pool—I wade, you dive—
while your golden retriever Ollie paces around us:
he thinks we're going to drown,
but he's scared of the blown-up alligator
and backs away when it gets too close.
We splash and kick
as plums drop into the pool—*plonk*—
then sit on the hot flagstones,
drink Diet Coke and talk about poetry.
You pull out weeds by their roots,
and set down the sprinkler so that arcs of water
fan out over the garden.
We eat under the Cinzano umbrella.
Ollie noses his head onto your lap.
You save a crust of your sandwich
and he snaps it up.
A screen door creaks and slams.
Your cat trots over the hot terrace
and streaks into the cool dark house.
We look at *People* magazine—all the starlets the same:
halter tops and hot red lips.
Reading Thoreau and Li Po.
Forgetting my father. Yours.
Fred's tests. My sister's blood clot in surgery.
Talking about your exes. Mine.
Saying we look pretty good for our age.
Loving your old baggy flowered bathing suit

that billows when you swim. Your hair
that falls onto your forehead and you push it back.
Pages of magazines flick in the wind.
Fred sings and plays his guitar—his voice floats outdoors,
then fades away again.
A yellow jacket worries around our plates:
you languidly swat it away.
Dropping strawberries into our mouths.
Smelling your roses: *Graham Thomas,*
Zephirine, Keep Smiling, Missing You.

Mud Lake

1

It's been eighteen years since I camped here every summer.
Yarrow and phlox are thick in the meadow.
My thighs brush against spirea
and Labrador tea.
Peter is dead, who camped here with me.
Backswimmer beetles still scull in the pond.
Willows still shake in the wind.
I miss this life.
I find my old pen, not much faded
from thirty years of snowpack and snowmelt.
Year after year I watched dragonfly larvae
climb out of the lake
like shaggy pennies covered with silt,
hang backwards on a rock,
foam into glittering engines,
then speed off into the forest.
Cowbells jangled
as cattle moved through the meadow.
After a storm,
mashed tiger lilies,
pollen floating in puddles,
pellets of melted hail,
and the smell of Mules' Ears and wet dust.
This year arrow-shaped leaves of Sagittaria
drift in the water.
Sedges begin to fill in the lake:
it's duller, muddier.
In another thirty years it will become a meadow.
No one will remember the stars that blurred in its water.

2

These lodgepole pines came up to my knees.
Now they're twenty feet high:
their reflections wobble in the shallows.
I see myself drilling into the granite of my past.
I've never turned away from it.
None of it meant as much to me as these red firs.
I think back to when I had that health and strength:
sketching corn lilies in their sheaths,
wading through brush to get to water,
digging up wild onions with my Swiss army knife for dinner.
Every evening a nighthawk boomed over the lake.
The logs are still covered with bark beetle tracks.
Dragonflies still flicker through the woods and land on my spoon.
I was so clear and sure:
I'd stare at midges as they swarmed in the sun,
watch a garter snake slacken and drop into the water.

3

My eyebrows are turning white,
even my pubic hair where Peter would rest his palm
as if listening. We made love by a brackish pond
as warblers flitted in and out of dead branches.
At night one white boulder blazed under the moon.
The constellations leaned down on their stalks.
Snow slumped off the pines and slid into the water.
Bug spray, mosquitoes, blackbirds, basalt.
Miles from the highway. Waking up in the morning
watching shadows of branches flickering across my tent.
I never thought I'd have years of sickness, being alone.
I never thought I'd want to slip back into my thirty-year-old body.
I want to be that strong and ignorant. Smell pine needles and snowmelt.
Listen to an alderfly land on my tin cup with a faint ring.

After Reading About the Next World

A psychic describes the next world as perfect, odorless, always
78 degrees. There is no sex, food, or death, and works of art
and buildings appear instantly, made manifest by thought.

I want to say a word for *this* world,
even though it's true everything is worn or wrong,
even sex is awkward, our bodies folded around an answer
which we blurt out, startled, like a student in the back of the
    class.
But what would we do if straw hats never frayed?
What about rust? What about lint?
What about hair in a sink drain,
the small wasted efforts at a poem,
the rasp of a crow, squeak of a faucet through walls at night,
a dog racing around after being hosed and shampooed
and shaking drops right into your eyes?
In *that* world leaves stay on their stems
and don't hiss in the wind, and there's no wind, or even rain, for
    that matter.
What if you wanted to see rain glazing the recycling bottles?
Smell the mold on an old plank or a washrag?
This morning I watched you cut sprouts off a potato:
there was dirt under your fingernails
when you opened my shirt and stroked my breasts;
when you touched my face, your hands smelled of potato.

I Lay on a Footbridge Over a Stream

Because the night scoured me,
took my little bundle of suffering,
filled me with clean black cold.
Sorrel and phlox. Smell of creosote.

All the pores of leaves closed, but I was open:
soaked by the dark. Shocked by the stars,
their astringent perfume.

Breathing

I love to feel as if I'm just another body, a breather along with
    the others:
blackbirds taking sips of air, garter snakes
lapping it up with their split tongues,
and all those plants
that open and close and throw up streamers of oxygen:
maybe that cottonwood that tilts across the creekbed
is the very one that just sucked up carbon dioxide
and let me breathe, maybe I should hang a card around it,
Thank you for the next two minutes of my life,
maybe some of the air I just swallowed used to be inside the hot
    larynx of a fox,
or the bill of an ash-throated flycatcher,
maybe it just coursed past
the scales of a lizard—a blue-belly—
as he wrapped himself around his mate,
maybe he took an extra breath and let it out
and that's the one I got.
Maybe all of us are standing side by side on the earth
our chests moving up and down,
every single one of us, opening a window,
loosening a belt, unzipping a pair of pants to let our bellies swell,
while in the pond a water beetle
clips a bubble of air to its shell and comes back up for another.
You want sanitary? Go to some other planet:
I'm breathing the same air as the drunk Southerner,
the one who rolls cigarettes with stained yellow thumbs
on the bench in the train station,
I'm breathing the same air as the Siamese twins
at the circus, their heads talking to each other,

quarreling about what they want to do with their one pair of
    hands
and their one heart.
Tires have run over this air,
it's passed right over the stiff hair of jackrabbits and roadkill,
drifted through clouds of algae and cumulus,
passed through jetprops,
blades of helicopters,
through spiderlings that balloon over the Tetons,
through sudden masses of smoke and sulfur,
the bleared Buick filled with smoke
from the Lucky Strikes my mother lit, one after another.
Though, as a child, I tried my best *not* to breathe,
I wanted to take only the faintest sips,
just enough to keep the sponges inside,
all the lung sacs, rising and falling.
I have never noticed it enough,
this colorless stuff I can't see,
circulated by fans, pumped into tires,
sullenly exploding into bubbles of marsh gas,
while the man on the gurney drags it in and out of his lungs
until it leaves his corpse and floats past doorknobs
and gets trapped in an ice cube, dropped into a glass.
After all, we're just hanging out here in our sneakers
or hooves or talons, gripping a branch, or thudding against the
    sidewalk:
as I hold onto my lover
and both of us breathe in the smell of wire screens on the
    windows
and the odor of buckeye.
This isn't to say I haven't had trouble breathing, I have:
sometimes I have to pull the car over and roll down the window,
and take in air, I have to remember I'm an animal,

I have to breathe with the other breathers,
even the stars breathe, even the soil,
even the sun is breathing up there,
all that helium and oxygen,
all those gases blowing and shredding into the solar wind.

Notes and Acknowledgments

"Practicing the Truth"—section 3 refers to constellations in the night sky: the Archer, the Arrow, the Eagle, and the Swan.

"You Ask What Saved Me"—the Lion and the Square are constellations.

"What Rises in the Sea at Night Rises in Dreams"—"shines like silver fire" by N.J. Berrill from *The Life of the Ocean* (McGraw-Hill, 1966).

"Long Distance: England"—"inhaling the smell of dusty cretonne" echoes a sentence from "Eveline," by James Joyce, from *Dubliners* (Dover Publications, 1991).

"Abuse: Reconsidering the Strategy of Silence"—"I want to walk under the sky with its black lock of silence/Count the stars with all their keys" echoes lines from " The New Apartment: Minneapolis" by Linda Hogan, from *Savings* (Coffee House Press, 1988).

"Summer at Barbara's House" and "Breathing" owe much to "Singing Back the World" and "Kissing," by Dorianne Laux, from *What We Carry* (Boa Editions Ltd., 1994).

I wish to thank the editors of the following journals and books, in which some of these poems first appeared, sometimes in different versions:

> *Barnabe Mountain Review, The Common Review, Connotation Press: An Online Artifact, Inquiring Mind, One (More) Glass, Orion, Pequod, Poetry, Runes, The Poet's Companion* (Norton), *Poetry International, Spoon River Poetry Review, The Sun, Witness,* and *84 Over 60: Women Poets on Love* (Mayapple Press).

A group of poems won the 1996 Paumanok Poetry Award from SUNY. "Mud Lake" won the 2011 Poetry International Prize.

I'm grateful to Chana Bloch and Kathleen Fraser for their encouragement and editorial help; to Alicia Ostriker for choosing my manuscript; to Michael Simms, for his dedication to poetry; and to the Autumn House staff, for all they do.

Special thanks to my writing group: Gerald Fleming, Bill Edmondson, Judith Serin, and Peter Kunz. Thanks also to the Marin Arts Council, Blue Mountain Center, Headlands Center for the Arts, and Ucross Foundation, which awarded me fellowships.

Gratitude always to Don Sandner, Marcia Anderson, Jackie Dennis, Barbara Bloom, and Valerie Cook. Many thanks to G.S., E.M.G., G.R., H.D., L.E., and S.G.

The Autumn House Poetry Series

Michael Simms, General Editor

• Winner of the annual Autumn House Poetry Prize

* *Coal Hill Review* chapbook series

Design and Production

Text and cover design: Chiquita Babb

Cover painting: "Mysterious Boat" by Odilon Redon

Photograph of cover painting: © Sotheby's/akg-images

Author photograph: Stephanie Mohan

This book was typeset in Stempel Garamond, a font released in 1925 by D. Stempel AG. The design of Stempel Garamond was based on a Claude Garamond roman shown in a 1592 speciment sheet by printer Egenolff-Berner, making it a genuine revival of Garamond's original typeface. Display elements were typeset in Lilith, a late twentieth-century font created by type designer and composer David Rakowski.

This book was printed by McNaughton & Gunn on 55# Glatfelter Natural.